S0-BYS-101

Community Helpers

Nurses

by Dee Ready

Reading Consultant:
Marie Griffin, RN, C
Member of the American Nurses Association

Bridgestone Books
an Imprint of Capstone Press

Bridgestone Books are published by Capstone Press
1710 Roe Crest Drive, North Mankato, Minnesota 56003
www.capstonepub.com

Copyright © 1997 by Capstone Press, a Capstone imprint. All rights reserved.
No part of this publication may be reproduced without written permission from the publisher.
The publisher takes no responsibility for the use of any of the materials
or methods described in this book, nor for the products thereof.

Library of Congress Cataloging-in-Publication Data
Ready, Delores.
    Nurses/by Dee Ready.
    p. cm.—(Community helpers)
    Includes bibliographical references and index.
    Summary: Explains the clothing, tools, schooling, and work of nurses.
    ISBN-13: 978-1-56065-512-1 (hardcover)
    ISBN-10: 1-56065-512-7 (hardcover)
    ISBN-13: 978-0-7368-8458-7 (softcover pbk.)
    ISBN-10: 0-7368-8458-0 (softcover pbk.)
    1. Nurses—Juvenile literature. [1. Nurses. 2. Occupations.] I. Title. II. Series:
    Community helpers (Mankato, Minn.)
RT61.5.R43 1997
610.78'06'9—dc21

                                        96-48636
                                          CIP
                                          AC

Photo credits

International Stock/James Davis, cover; Ronn Maratea, 8, 10;
Michael Philip
  Manheim, 18
FPG/Jeff Kaufman, 4, 6, 12; Art Montes De Oca, 16
Unicorn/Tom McCarthhy, 14
Visuals Unlimited/Jeff Greenberg, 20

Printed in the United States of America in North Mankato, Minnesota.
022012   006608

Table of Contents

Nurses 5

What Nurses Do 7

Different Kinds of Nurses 9

What Nurses Wear 11

Tools Nurses Use 13

Nurses and School 15

Where Nurses Work 17

People Who Help Nurses 19

Nurses Help Others 21

Hands On: Test Your Heart Rate 22

Words to Know 23

Read More 24

Internet Sites 24

Index 24

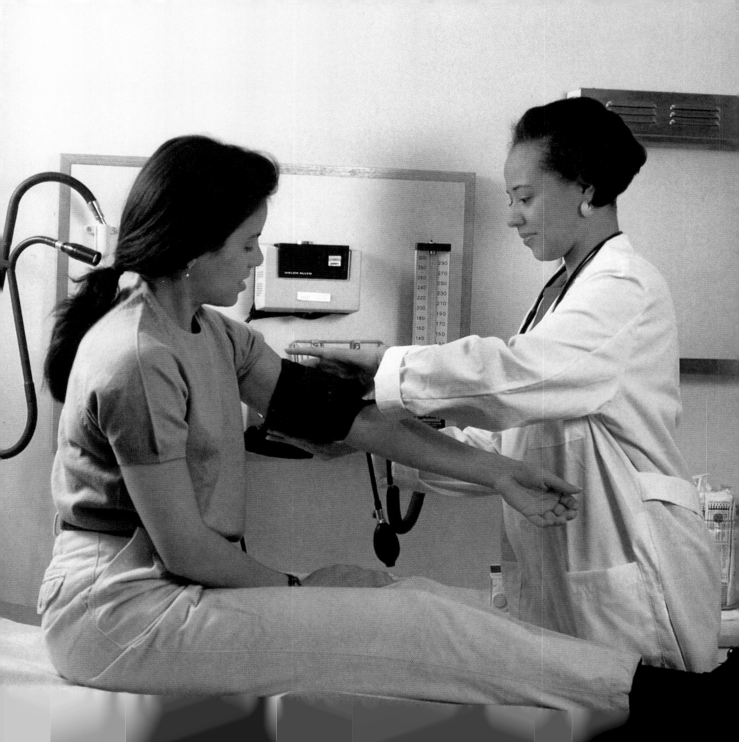

Nurses

Nurses help people who are sick. They check a patient's vital signs. The vital signs are pulse, breathing, temperature, and blood pressure. Nurses help doctors in hospitals and clinics.

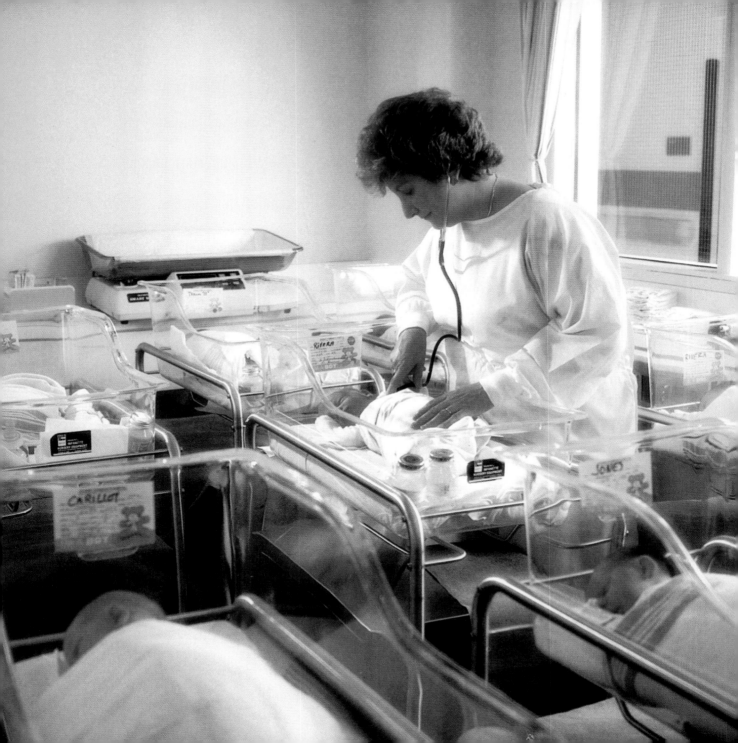

What Nurses Do

Nurses ask patients questions about their symptoms. A symptom is a sign of illness. Nurses also take care of people who are sick. They feed and watch over newborn babies, too.

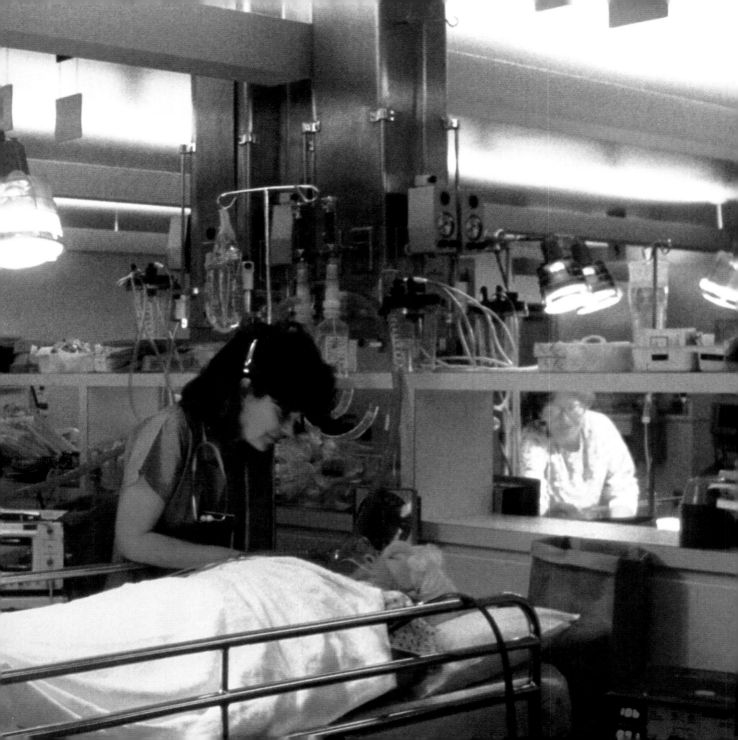

Different Kinds of Nurses

Some nurses help people in the emergency room. Other nurses help people who are having an operation. An operation is cutting open part of the body to fix a problem. School nurses help children who are hurt at school.

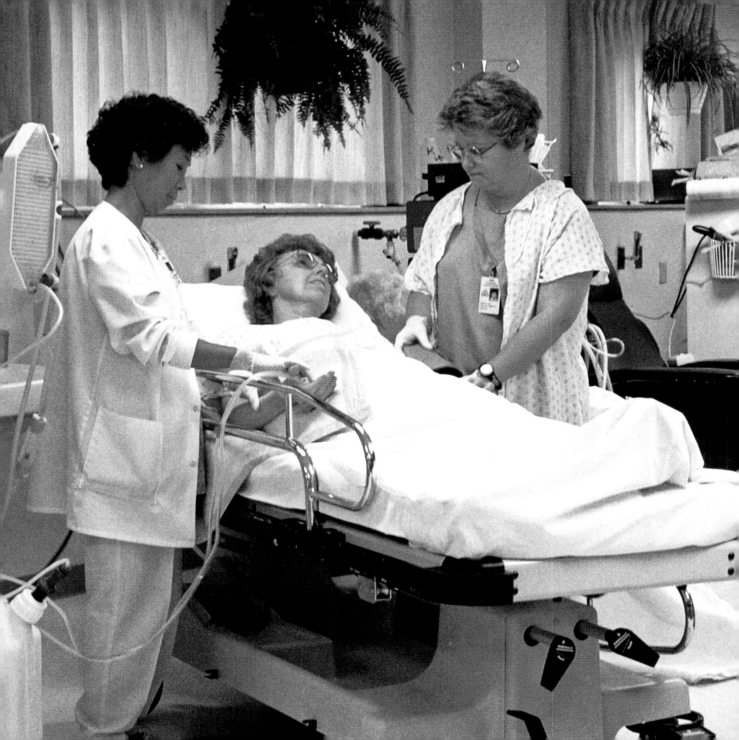

What Nurses Wear

Most nurses wear white uniforms and white shoes. Some nurses working in the hospital wear scrubs. Scrubs are loose-fitting shirts and pants.

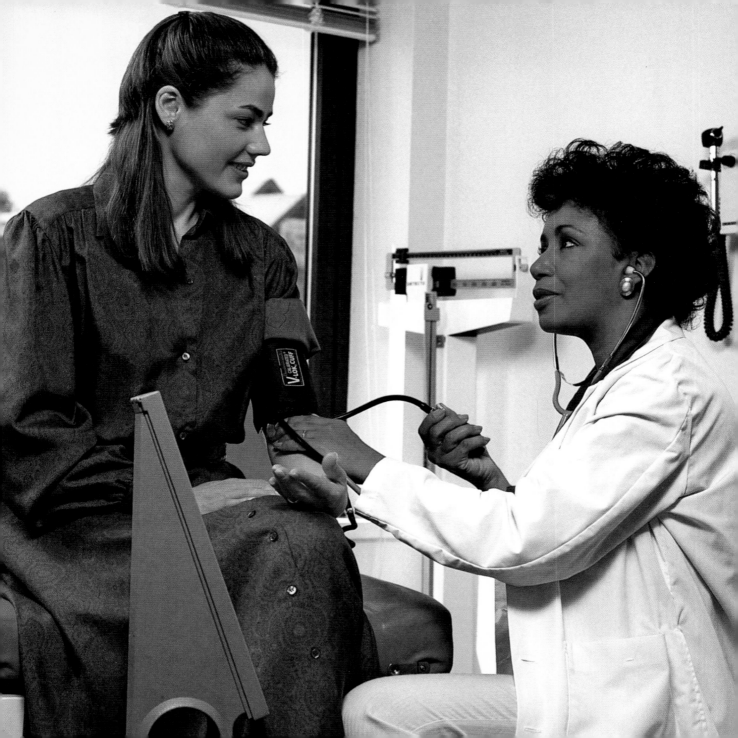

Tools Nurses Use

Nurses measure a patient's blood pressure with a cuff. They check a patient's temperature with a thermometer. They listen to a patient's heartbeat and breathing with a stethoscope.

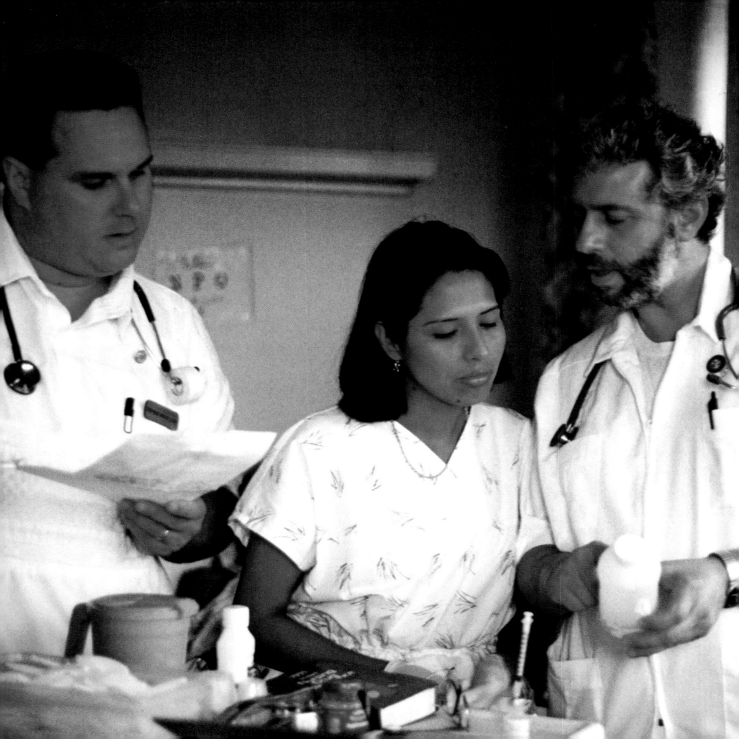

Nurses and School

Students study nursing in college for three to five years. They learn in classrooms and in hospitals. Student nurses have hands-on training with real patients. They must pass a test called boards before they can work as nurses.

Where Nurses Work

Emergency-room and operating-room nurses work in hospitals. Home-care nurses visit people in their homes. Some nurses work in clinics. Others work at schools or factories.

People Who Help Nurses

Nurses need other people to help them do their jobs. Doctors operate on patients and tell nurses what medicines to give them. Nurse's aides bathe and feed patients.

Nurses Help Others

Patients are the first concern of nurses. Nurses are taught to see a patient's illness. They are also taught to see their feelings. They want patients to be happy and healthy.

Hands On: Test Your Heart Rate

Your heart is always pumping. Sometimes it pumps faster than at other times. It pumps faster when you are active. Your heart pumps slower when you are sitting still. You can test your heart rate to see how fast and slow it can be.

1. Sit still for five minutes. Relax like you are about to go to sleep.

2. Find your pulse. Your pulse is the steady beat of your heart as it moves blood through your body. You can find your pulse on the side of your neck.

3. Find the second hand on a watch or on a clock. Count how many times your heart beats in six seconds.

4. Add a zero to the end of the number. This is the number of beats your heart makes in one minute. Write the number down.

5. Now run as fast as you can. Then stop and count your heart rate again using the same steps.

6. Compare the two numbers. Your heart works harder when you are exercising. It slows down when you are still. Try other activities to see how your heart rate changes.

Words to Know

clinic (KLIN-ik)—an office where people go for a medical exam

patient (PAY-shuhnt)—a person who receives medical care

pulse (PUHLSS)—the steady beat of your heart as it moves blood through your body

stethoscope (STETH-uh-skope)—a medical tool used to listen to the sounds of a patient's chest

symptom (SIMP-tuhm)—a sign of illness

thermometer (thur-MOM-uh-tur)—a tool used to measure temperature

vital signs (VYE-tuhl SINZ)—the signs that show there is life

Read More

Burby, Lisa N. *A Day in the Life of a Nurse*. New York: PowerKids Press, 1999.

Flanagan, Alice K. *Ask Nurse Pfaff, She'll Help You!* Our Neighborhood. New York: Children's Press, 1997.

Internet Sites

FactHound offers a safe, fun way to find Internet sites related to this book. All of the sites on FactHound have been researched by our staff.

Here's all you do:
Visit *www.facthound.com*
Type in this code: 9781560655121

Index

blood pressure, 5, 13
boards, 15
breathing, 5, 13
clinic, 5, 17
doctor, 5, 19
emergency room, 9, 17
hospital, 5, 11, 15, 17
medicine, 19
newborns, 7

nurse's aide, 19
operation, 9
patient, 5, 7, 13, 15, 19, 21
pulse, 5
school, 9, 15, 17
scrubs, 11
stethoscope, 13
thermometer, 13
vital signs, 5